Story and pictures by JEANETTE WINTER

She died—<u>this</u> was the way she died.
And when her breath was done
Took up her simple wardrobe
And started for the sun.
Her little figure at the gate
The Angels must have spied,
Since I could never find her
Upon the mortal side.

Emily Dickinson's

Letters

to the

World

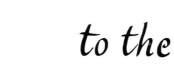

FRANCES FOSTER BOOKS
FARRAR, STRAUS AND GIROUX
New York

My sister Emily was buried today.

The spring sun dried the tears
that ran down
my cheeks.

Emily's upstairs room
was the smallest in the house.

On many a night
her lamp burned bright
until dawn.
What kept Emily awake,
we wondered?

Emily never went anywhere.
Townsfolk thought her strange.

This house—and the garden—
were her world.

Emily's writing table is bare now.

Where are the sheets
and scraps of paper
she was always
writing on?

Emily read the dictionary
as others read a storybook.

What did Emily find
in all those
words?

And here are the dresses she wore—
only white—in summer and winter.

But, oh! what is this?
Poems—and poems—
and even more poems—
there must be hundreds!
This, then, is what Emily was writing—
day and night, it must have been.

"This is my letter to the World..."

This is my letter to the World
That never wrote to Me—
The simple News that Nature told—
With tender Majesty

Her Message is committed
To Hands I cannot see—
For love of Her—Sweet—countrymen—
Judge tenderly—of Me

This is my letter to the World
That never wrote to Me—
The simple News that Nature told—
With tender Majesty

Her Message is committed
To Hands I cannot see—
For love of Her—Sweet—countrymen—
Judge tenderly—of Me

It *was* the brave Columbus,
A sailing o'er the tide,
Who notified the nations
Of where I would reside!

Snow flakes.

I counted till they danced so
Their slippers leaped the town,
And then I took a pencil
To note the rebels down.
And then they grew so jolly
I did resign the prig,
And ten of my once stately toes
Are marshalled for a jig!

I'm Nobody! Who are you?
Are you—Nobody—Too?
Then there's a pair of us!
Don't tell! they'd advertise—you know!

How dreary—to be—Somebody!
How public—like a Frog—
To tell one's name—the livelong June—
To an admiring Bog!

I started Early—Took my Dog—
And visited the Sea—
The Mermaids in the Basement
Came out to look at me—

And Frigates—in the Upper Floor
Extended Hempen Hands—
Presuming Me to be a Mouse—
Aground—upon the Sands—

The Way I read a Letter's—this—
'Tis first—I lock the Door—
And push it with my fingers—next—
For transport it be sure—

And then I go the furthest off
To counteract a knock—
Then draw my little Letter forth
And slowly pick the lock—

Have you got a Brook in your little heart,
Where bashful flowers blow,
And blushing birds go down to drink,
And shadows tremble so—

And nobody knows, so still it flows,
That any brook is there,
And yet your little draught of life
Is daily drunken there—

'Twas such a little—little boat
That toddled down the bay!
'Twas such a gallant—gallant sea
That beckoned it away!

'Twas such a greedy, greedy wave
That licked it from the Coast—
Nor ever guessed the stately sails
My little craft was <u>lost</u>!

I stepped from Plank to Plank
A slow and cautious way
The Stars about my Head I felt
About my Feet the Sea.

I knew not but the next
Would be my final inch—
This gave me that precarious Gait
Some call Experience.

A Spider sewed at Night
Without a Light
Upon an Arc of White.

Where Ships of Purple—gently toss—
On Seas of Daffodil—
Fantastic Sailors—mingle—
And then—the Wharf is still!

To make a prairie it takes a clover
      and one bee,
One clover, and a bee,
And revery.
The revery alone will do,
If bees are few.

The Moon was but a Chin of Gold
A Night or two ago—
And now she turns Her perfect Face
Upon the World below—

Her Bonnet is the Firmament—
The Universe—Her Shoe—
The Stars—the Trinkets at Her Belt—
Her Dimities—of Blue—

Will there really be a "Morning"?
Is there such a thing as "Day"?
Could I see it from the mountains
If I were as tall as they?

Has it feet like Water lilies?
Has it feathers like a Bird?
Is it brought from famous countries
Of which I have never heard?

Oh some Scholar! Oh some Sailor!
Oh some Wise Man from the skies!
Please to tell a little Pilgrim
Where the place called "Morning" lies!

If I can stop one Heart from breaking
I shall not live in vain
If I can ease one Life the Aching
Or cool one Pain

Or help one fainting Robin
Unto his Nest again
I shall not live in Vain.

Could I but ride indefinite
As doth the Meadow Bee
And visit only where I liked
And No one visit me

And flirt all Day with Buttercups
And marry whom I may
And dwell a little everywhere
Or better, run away

Some keep the Sabbath going to Church—
I keep it, staying at Home—
With a Bobolink for a Chorister—
And an Orchard, for a Dome—

There is no Frigate like a Book
To take us Lands away
Nor any Coursers like a Page
Of prancing Poetry—

I never saw a Moor—
I never saw the Sea—
Yet know I how the Heather looks
And what a Billow be.

Exultation is the going
Of an inland soul to sea,
Past the houses—past the headlands—
Into deep Eternity—

"Hope" is the thing with feathers—
That perches in the soul—
And sings the tune without the words—
And never stops—at all—

Emily, the world *will* read your letter—
your poems.

NOTE

Emily Dickinson was born in 1830, in Amherst, Massachusetts. When she was nine years old, the family moved to a red brick house on North Pleasant Street, where Emily lived the rest of her life. Her sister, Lavinia, discovered the poems after her death in 1886.

Emily Dickinson left behind 1,775 poems, most of them unpublished during her lifetime. Today she is recognized as a pioneer in American poetry.

A sheltered life can be a daring life as well.
For all serious daring starts from within.
—Eudora Welty

To Max

Copyright © 2002 by Jeanette Winter
All rights reserved
Distributed in Canada by Douglas & McIntyre Ltd.
Text type set in Cloister Oldstyle
Lettering by Judythe Sieck
Color separations by Hong Kong Scanner Arts
Printed and bound in the United States by Berryville Graphics
Designed by Jeanette Winter and Judythe Sieck
First edition, 2002
10 9 8 7 6 5 4 3 2 1

Library of Congress Cataloging-in-Publication Data
Winter, Jeanette.
    Emily Dickinson's letters to the world / story and
illustrations by Jeanette Winter.— 1st ed.
        p.   cm.
    Includes selections from the poetry of Emily Dickinson.
    Summary: A brief description of the life of Emily Dickinson
and a selection of her poems.
    ISBN 0-374-32147-7
    1. Dickinson, Emily, 1830–1886–Juvenile literature.
    2. Poets, American–19th century–Biography–Juvenile literature.
    3. Children's poetry, American. [1. Dickinson, Emily, 1830–1886.
    2. Poets, American. 3. Women–Biography. 4. American poetry.]
    I. Dickinson, Emily, 1830–1886. II. Title.

PS1541.Z5 W55 2002
811'.4–dc21
[B]
                                                    2001033277

Poetry used by permission of the publishers and the
Trustees of Amherst College from *The Poems of Emily Dickinson*,
Thomas H. Johnson, ed., Cambridge, Mass.: The Belknap Press of
Harvard University Press, Copyright © 1951, 1955, 1979, 1983 by the
President and Fellows of Harvard College.